THE BUNYIP AND THE NIGHT

*The river is too deep, child, and the
Bunyip lives in the water under the
stones.*

From: **Geoffrey Hamlyn** *by Henry Kingsley*

*m*ark *n*estor *s*vendsen

*"I remember when first Bunyips were real. It was just after I discovered
that nothing was real and, if nothing was real, dreams were as true as
anything else. As a child I dreamed a lot and I remember the first time
with Bunyips . . . It was during a camping trip to Carnarvon Gorge. At
Carnarvon the sandstone walls tower like a cathedral. The road drops
from the dry land into the cool and sculptured green. And there is water
there, in abundance, clear water winking past smooth rocks. But mostly
there are dreams, very old dreams, dreams of fierce integrity; so old and
so powerful that walkers into the valley become part of that dreaming.
The spirits are not quiet here, they whisper and chatter from the cliffs. It
was here the Bunyips first found me as they hid in the pools; at dusk they
moved behind fire black trees and wailed like curlews, or dingos, in the
two sided valley.*

*Since then Bunyips, the manifestations of fear in us all, have been with
me. Now I know them they are not so bad, though there're new ones all
the time. Some of them are old companions, almost friendly really . . ."*

**Mark Nestor Svendsen was born in Yeppoon and now lives in Zilzie,
Emu Park where he writes things.**

THE BUNYIP AND THE NIGHT

by

***m**ark **n**estor **s**vendsen*

illustrated by

***a**nnmarie **s**cott*
***a**rone **r**aymond **m**eeks*
***n**arelle **o**liver*
***g**eoffrey **e**lliott*
***d**avid **m**ackintosh*
***a**rmin **g**reder*

JamRoll
UQP
Children's Book
Publishers

THE BUNYIP

illustrated by annmarie scott

*B*unyip crawls on the wild wind hill,
And loud he roars both fierce and chill.
Or was it the wind? I could have sworn,
I heard the door rattle and the frost-snapping lawn,
Crunch to the crushing-up, wolfing-down tread,
Of the Bunyip lurking just around behind the shed.

Just beyond the safety of the yellow light door,
The Bunyip is lurking with his deadening claw!

So snuggle up, cuddle up, sleep warm in bed
Coz if the Bunyip gets you . . .

. . . you'll be dead,

Dead,

DEAD!

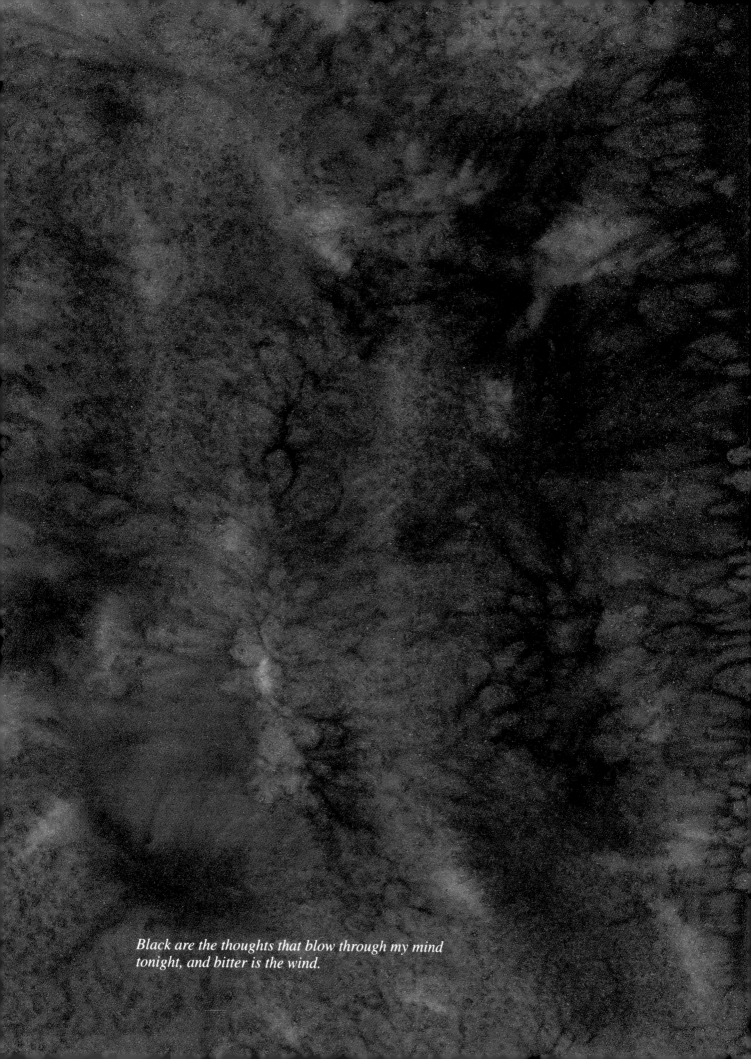

*Black are the thoughts that blow through my mind
tonight, and bitter is the wind.*

THE BUNYIP WAILS

illustrated by

arone raymond meeks

*I*n the City there's no Bunyips,
At least they tell me so,
But when the bitter night nips,
The shadows start to flow . . .

In the cold snouted moonlight,
With the stars sharp and bright,
There are fell,
There are fell,
Things lurking in the night.

At the dark edge of midnight,
When blackened is all sight,
I can tell,
I can tell;
Though I pray with all my might;
I can tell,
I can tell;
That something isn't right.

Can you hear the Bunyip wailing near the highway far away?
While the huge bellied darkness chuckles mercilessly, aiee!
Until your city cousins say to you,
"That ambulance is near."
And that stops all your trembling,
And puts aside your fear.

But still you can't help wondering,
What murder, mayhem, woe
Is there happening in the city streets,
Where ambulances go?

The Bunyip dragged from its slimey hole.
"I go to snare the child," it said.
"Remember us," cried the slimmering
eels, "for hunger gnaws your brothers."

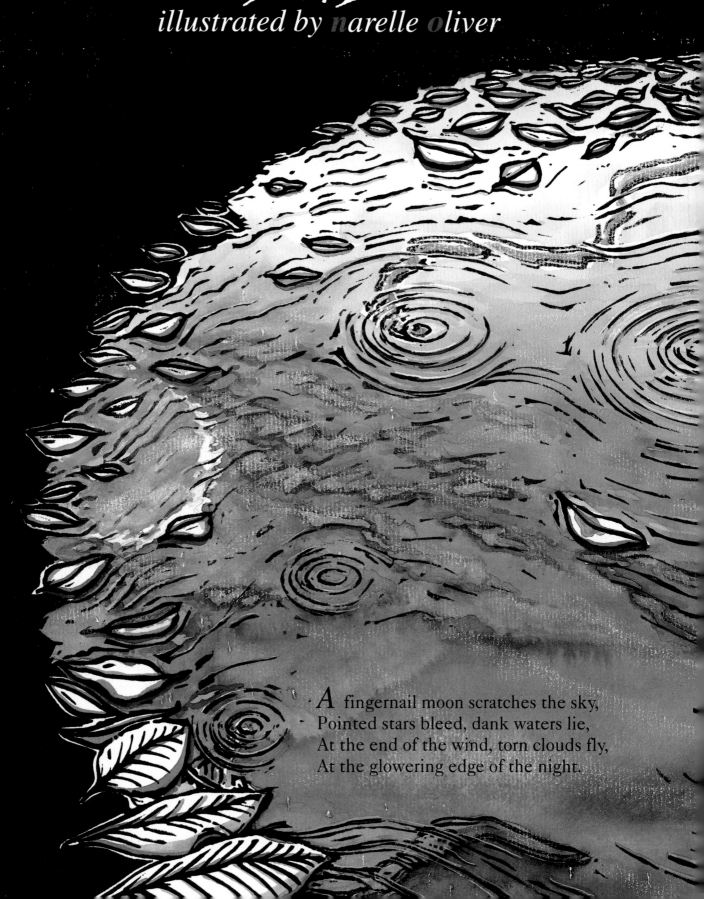

THE BUNYIP AND THE NIGHT

illustrated by *narelle oliver*

A fingernail moon scratches the sky,
Pointed stars bleed, dank waters lie,
At the end of the wind, torn clouds fly,
At the glowering edge of the night.

Hunger gnawed the Bunyip sings,
Of the black, of the night, of fear filled things,
Of the visible dark, unsettlings,
By the glowing edge of the night.

The morning dries the various stars,
Melts the iced night where they are,
But where goes the black? Where go the bars,
Of the cage of the visible night?

They are there in the depths of deep black alleys,
There in billabongs and dark valleys,
There in minds where dreams are carried,
The small black hearts of the night.

But the one eyed evening ends the day,
The dark crawls out from where it lay,
Devours the light that's in its way,
Re-builds the house of the night.

The dark drools out like Bunyip spittle,
Night is black, day dreams brittle,
But soon comes sleep, rest a little,
And dream in the eyes of the Bunyip,
In the blackened eyes of the Bunyip,
In the visible eyes of the Bunyip,
In the dark sweet house of your dreams.

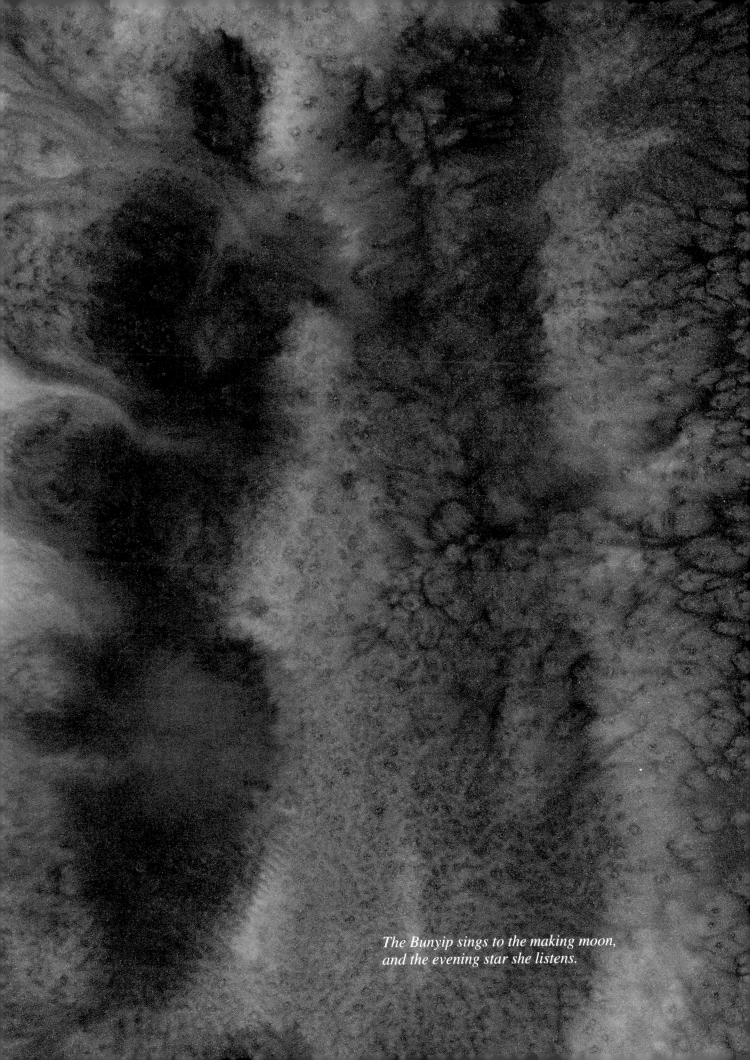

The Bunyip sings to the making moon,
and the evening star she listens.

THE BUNYIP SLEEPS

illustrated by

geoffrey elliott

*B*unyip stalks through the huddled, cluttered town,
When the moon is set and the lights are down.
To the yammer of the dogs and the spit fire cats,
In the dark, with the lonely-fanged, hell fire bats.

Bunyip moves through black hush of the night,
Wakes plovers that scream as they start in fright.
To the desolate, uttermost edge of the town,
There the Bunyip stops and shudders and frowns.

For the sun's rolling up setting spikes in the sky,
And the Bunyip wails for a place to lie.
Who has walked in the night, where will rest ever be,
Where the small waves tremble at the corners of the sea?

O children lie warm curled like flowers in their beds,
Dreams like moths brush and fluttering through their heads,
But where is the bed that the Bunyip needs?
In the dank, black waterhole drowned with the weeds.

Let the day birds laugh, breathe the morning in,
Like death is the yellow light, clamour and din,
To the Bunyip loveless is the sun,
To the patches of night let the Bunyip run.

As the flying fox folds the dark with her wings,
So the Bunyip sinks as the rooster sings.
Look for him there where the ripples rise,
Where tea trees droop Bunyip closes his eyes.

There let his black heart lie at rest,
Dreaming dreams that you and I detest.
There leave him lie, undisturbed let him be,
In the tender dark he loves, Bunyip's dreams drift free.

Recipe for Bunyip Soup

Slime of eel,
Wing of bat,
Baby's finger –
"Must have that!"
Cheeping chickens,
From the coop,
Boiling water,
Bunyip Soup!

THERE'S
BUNYIPS

illustrated by

david **m**ackintosh

*T*here's Bunyips under my pillow,
Bunyips under my bed,

Bunyips between my sheets you know,
They're gnawing at something dead.

Bunyips lurk around corners,
Loll in the shade behind doors,

Make themselves look just like school uniforms,
Hung in the night on my drawers.

But I sneer at the scrattling Bunyips,
Wherever they are in my room,

I laugh in their faces, so they know their places,
My water glass drips out their doom . . . coz

Everybody knows,
If Bunyips wet their toes,
They shrivel like leather,
And vanish forever,
Like smoke in the wind when it goes.

PS: *Any self respecting child reading these poems together will realise that in one of them a Bunyip sinks down into a pool. How is this so, given that if they wet their toes they will vanish? Simple, Bunyips descend to the bottoms of irksome pools head first leaving their toes just above the water. The easiest way to check if a pool has Bunyips is to check in the lank reeds for their clawsome toes. This exercise is not recommended however, because any downward pressure on their toes would kill them if the toes descended below the water. Because of this, touching a Bunyip's toes causes a reflex action as the furious Bunyip pushes off the bottom of the pool and out onto the bank gnashing and screaming his slimy, toothsome, hideous screams of fury. This is definitely NOT a recommended procedure.*

BUNYIP'S TEETH

illustrated by

a r m i n   g r e d e r

A Bunyip could do with a finger or two,
When lacking something nice to chew,
So don't tease the Bunyip whatever you do,
Or the finger might, belong to you.

This book is for
My darling Annie Shaw
Who lives with them.
M'dearest Thyri
Who has to, too,
And Hannah, the Mouse.

First published 1994 by University of Queensland Press
Box 42, St Lucia, Queensland 4067, Australia.

© Mark Nestor Svendsen
© Illustrations, Geoffrey Elliott, Armin Greder,
David Mackintosh, Arone Raymond Meeks, Narelle Oliver,
Annmarie Scott

Book design by Gregory Rogers

Typeset by Ocean Graphics Pty Ltd, Gold Coast, Queensland
Text set in Caslon 14/16

Produced by Mandarin Offset in Hong Kong
Printed in Hong Kong

Distributed in the USA and Canada by
International Specialized Book Services, Inc.,
5804 N.E. Hassalo Street, Portland, Oregon 97213-3640

Sponsored by Queensland Office of Arts and Cultural
Development

Cataloguing in Publication Data
National Library of Australia

Svendsen, Mark, 1962-   .
    The bunyip and the night.

ISBN 0 7022 2702 1.

1 Children's poetry, Australian. 2. Bunyips — Juvenile poetry.
I. Scott, Annmarie, 1968-   . II. Title. (Series: Jam roll).

ARTS QUEENSLAND

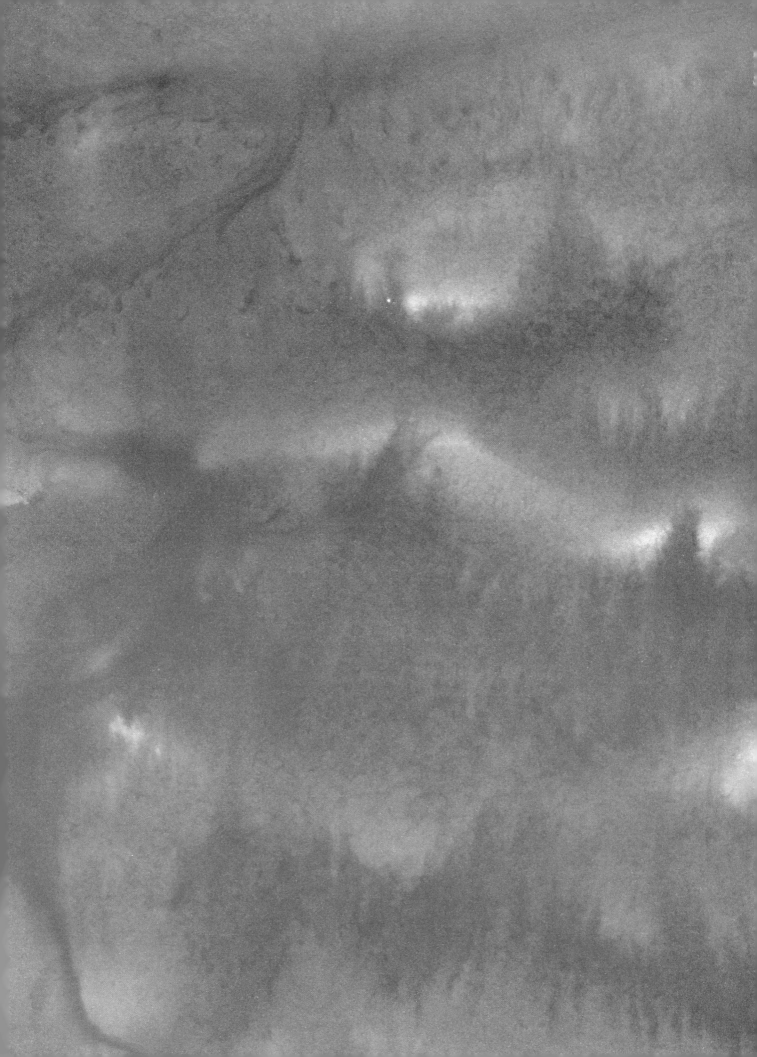